illustrated by
NIKO CHOCHELI

CHRIST in the OLD TESTAMENT
PROPHECY ILLUSTRATED

Compiled and edited by Thomas Hopko

ST VLADIMIR'S SEMINARY PRESS • CRESTWOOD • NEW YORK • 2002

Dedicated to
the blessed memory
of my great-grandparents,
the noted Georgian scientist
Solomon Kurdiani and his
dear wife Varvara.

—

The benefactors who made
this publication possible wish
to dedicate it in thanksgiving
for their children, Michael,
David, King,
Olivia, Karl
and Sophia.

Library of Congress
Cataloging-in-Publication Data

Bible. O.T. English. Revised Standard. Selections. 2002.
    Christ in the Old Testament: Prophecy illustrated /
    illustrated by Niko Chocheli.
        p. cm.
    ISBN 0-88141-237-6
        1. Jesus Christ—Biography—Sources, Biblical.
        1. Chocheli, Niko, 1968- II. Title.
BT299.2 .C525 2002
232'.12—dc21   2002017751

Christ in the Old Testament: Prophecy Illustrated

Illustrated by Niko Chocheli • Compiled & edited by Thomas Hopko

Copyright ©2002 ST VLADIMIR'S SEMINARY PRESS
575 Scarsdale Road, Crestwood, New York, 10707-1699
1-800-204-2665 • ISBN 0-88141-237-6

Scripture excerpts are taken from the New Oxford Annotated Bible,
Revised Standard Version, ©1973, with some alterations for clarity.

Book and cover design: Amber Houx
Text set in Goudy Thirty, Lanston Type Company

PRINTED IN CANADA

For as the rain and the
snow come down from
heaven, and return not
thither but water the
earth, making it
bring forth and
sprout, giving
seed to the
sower and
bread to the
eater, so shall
my word
be that
goes forth
from my
mouth; it shall
not return to me
empty, but it shall
accomplish that which
I purpose, and prosper
in the thing for which
I sent it.
                    Isaiah 55.10-11

And beginning with
Moses and all the
prophets, he interpreted
to them in all the
scriptures the things
concerning himself.
                    Luke 24.27

CREATOR OF THE WORLD

In the beginning God created the heavens and the earth. The earth was without form and void, and darkness was upon the face of the deep; and the Spirit of God was moving over the face of the waters. And God said, "Let there be light"; and there was light.

Genesis 1.1-3

In the beginning was the Word, and the Word was with God, and the Word was God. He was in the beginning with God; all things were made through him, and without him was not anything made that was made. In him was life, and the life was the light of men... And the Word became flesh and dwelt among us, full of grace and truth; we have beheld his glory, glory as of the only Son from the Father.

John 1.1-4 & 14

OLD ADAM AND NEW ADAM

Then God said, "Let us make man in our image, after our likeness... Then the Lord God formed man (adam) of dust from the ground (adama), and breathed into his nostrils the breath of life; and man became a living being.

Genesis 1.26 & 2.7

Thus it is written, "The first man Adam became a living being"; the last Adam (Christ) became a life-giving spirit... The first man was from the ground, a man of dust; the second man is from heaven... Just as we have born the image of the man of dust, we shall also bear the image of the man of heaven.

1 Corinthians 15.45, 47 & 49

GLORY OF GOD

Moses said, "I pray thee, show me thy glory." And the Lord said, "I will make all my goodness pass before you, and will proclaim before you my name 'The LORD.'" "But," he said, "you cannot see my face, for man shall not see me and live... While my glory passes by I will put you in the cleft of the rock... you shall see my back; but my face shall not be seen."

Exodus 33.18-23

"We have beheld his glory, glory as of the only Son from the Father... No one has ever seen God; the only Son, who is in the bosom of the Father, he has made him known."

John 1.14 & 18

For it is God who said, "Let light shine out of darkness," who has shone in our hearts to give the light of knowledge of the glory of God in the face of Christ.

2 Corinthians 4.6

SON OF DAVID

For thy servant David's sake do not turn away the face of thy anointed one. The Lord swore to David a sure oath from which he will not turn back: "One of the sons of your body I will set on your throne... There will I make a horn to sprout for David; I have prepared a lamp for my anointed. His enemies I will clothe with shame, but upon himself his crown will shed its luster."

Psalm 132.10-11 & 17-18

And as Jesus taught in the temple, he said, "How can the scribes say that the Christ is the son of David? David himself, inspired by the Holy Spirit, declared, 'The Lord said to my Lord, sit at my right hand, till I put thy enemies under thy feet.' David himself calls him Lord; so how is he his Son?"

Mark 12.35-37

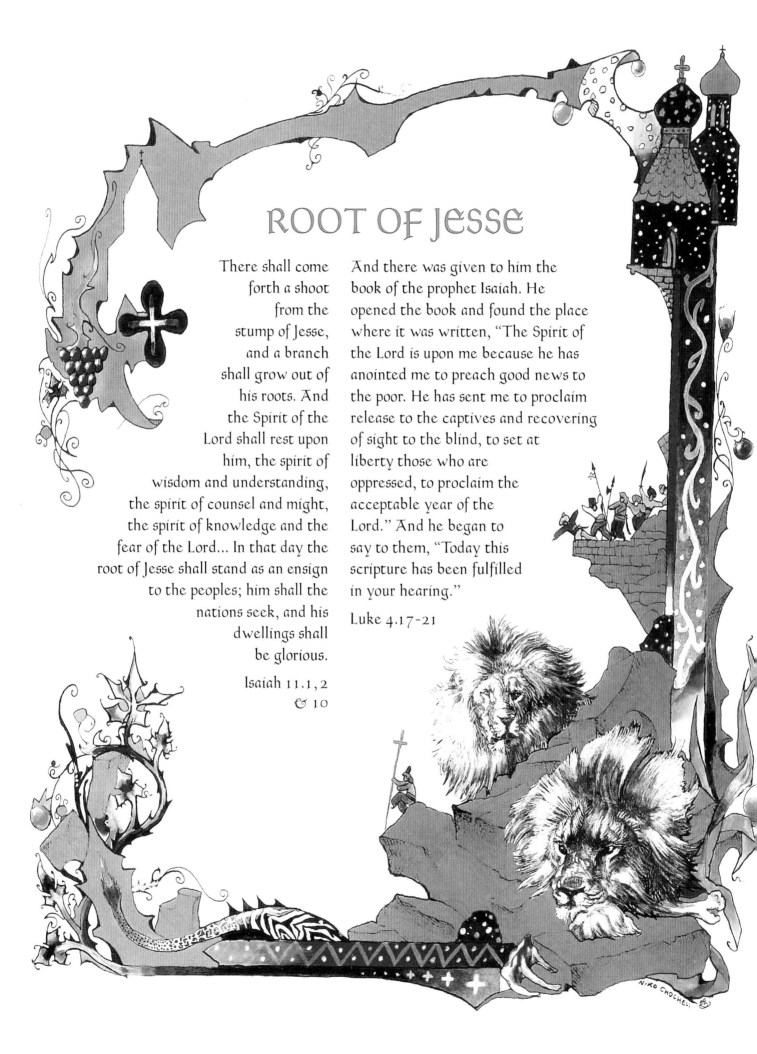

ROOT OF JESSE

There shall come forth a shoot from the stump of Jesse, and a branch shall grow out of his roots. And the Spirit of the Lord shall rest upon him, the spirit of wisdom and understanding, the spirit of counsel and might, the spirit of knowledge and the fear of the Lord... In that day the root of Jesse shall stand as an ensign to the peoples; him shall the nations seek, and his dwellings shall be glorious.

Isaiah 11.1, 2 & 10

And there was given to him the book of the prophet Isaiah. He opened the book and found the place where it was written, "The Spirit of the Lord is upon me because he has anointed me to preach good news to the poor. He has sent me to proclaim release to the captives and recovering of sight to the blind, to set at liberty those who are oppressed, to proclaim the acceptable year of the Lord." And he began to say to them, "Today this scripture has been fulfilled in your hearing."

Luke 4.17-21

THE VIRGIN SHALL CONCEIVE

Therefore the Lord himself will give you a sign. Behold the virgin shall conceive and bear a son, and shall call his name Immanuel.

Isaiah 7.14

"Joseph, son of David, do not fear to take Mary your wife, for that which is conceived in her is of the Holy Spirit; she will bear a son, and you shall call his name Jesus, for he will save his people from their sins." All this took place to fulfill what the Lord had spoken by the prophet: "Behold, a virgin shall conceive and bear a son, and his name shall be called Immanuel (which means, God with us).

Matthew 1.20-23

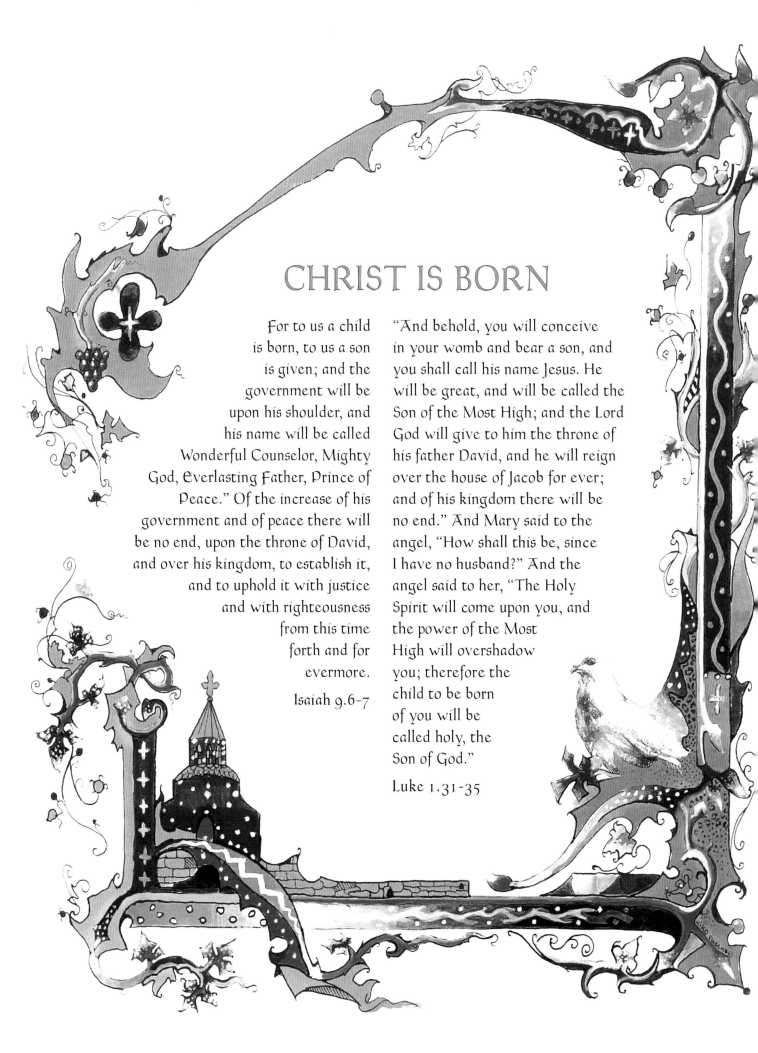

CHRIST IS BORN

For to us a child is born, to us a son is given; and the government will be upon his shoulder, and his name will be called Wonderful Counselor, Mighty God, Everlasting Father, Prince of Peace." Of the increase of his government and of peace there will be no end, upon the throne of David, and over his kingdom, to establish it, and to uphold it with justice and with righteousness from this time forth and for evermore.

Isaiah 9.6-7

"And behold, you will conceive in your womb and bear a son, and you shall call his name Jesus. He will be great, and will be called the Son of the Most High; and the Lord God will give to him the throne of his father David, and he will reign over the house of Jacob for ever; and of his kingdom there will be no end." And Mary said to the angel, "How shall this be, since I have no husband?" And the angel said to her, "The Holy Spirit will come upon you, and the power of the Most High will overshadow you; therefore the child to be born of you will be called holy, the Son of God."

Luke 1.31-35

BAPTISM IN THE JORDAN

When all Israel had finished passing over the Jordan, the Lord said to Joshua, "Take twelve men from the people, from each tribe a man, and command them, 'Take twelve stones from here out of the midst of the Jordan... Pass on before the ark of the Lord your God into the midst of the Jordan...' " Then... the waters of the Jordan were cut off before the ark of the covenant of the Lord; when it passed over the Jordan, the waters of the Jordan were cut off.

Joshua 4.1-7

The sea looked and fled, Jordan turned back.

Psalm 114.3

In those days came John the Baptist, preaching in the wilderness of Judea... [and] went out to him Jerusalem and all Judea and all the region about the Jordan, and they were baptized by him in the river Jordan, confessing their sins... Then Jesus came from Galilee to the Jordan to John, to be baptized by him... And when Jesus was baptized, he went up immediately from the water, and behold, the heavens were opened and he saw the Spirit of God descending like a dove, and alighting upon him; and lo, a voice from heaven saying, "This is my beloved Son with whom I am well pleased."

Matthew 3.1, 5-6, 13, & 16-17

LIGHT IN THE DARKNESS

He will make glorious the way of the sea, the land beyond the Jordan, Galilee of the nations. The people who walked in darkness have seen a great light; those who dwelt in a land of deep darkness, on them has light shined.

Isaiah 9.1-2

Leaving Nazareth Jesus went and dwelt in Capernaum by the sea, in the territory of Zebulun and Naphtali, that what was spoken by the prophet Isaiah might be fulfilled: "The land of Zebulun and of Naphtali, toward the sea, across the Jordan, Galilee of the Gentiles - the people who sat in darkness have seen a great light, and for those who sat in the region and shadow of death light has dawned."

Matthew 4.13-16

ENTRY INTO JERUSALEM

Rejoice greatly, O daughter of Zion! Shout aloud, O daughter of Jerusalem! Lo, your king comes to you; triumphant and victorious is he, humble and riding on an ass, on a colt of the foal of an ass.

Zechariah 9.9

The next day a great crowd who had come to the feast heard that Jesus was coming to Jerusalem. So they took branches of palm trees and went out to meet him, crying "Hosanna! Blessed is he who comes in the name of the Lord, even the King of Israel!" And Jesus found a young ass and sat upon it.

John 12.12-14

SUFFERING SERVANT

But he was wounded for our transgressions, he was bruised for our iniquities; upon him was the chastisement that made us whole, and with his wounds we are healed.

Isaiah 53.5

He bore our sins in his body on the tree, that we might die to sin and live in righteousness. By his wounds you have been healed. For you were straying sheep, but have now returned to the Shepherd and Guardian of your souls.

1 Peter 2.24-25

VICTORY OVER DEATH

He will swallow up death for ever, and the Lord God will wipe away tears from all faces...

Isaiah 25.8

Thy dead shall live, their bodies shall rise. O dwellers in the dust, awake and sing for joy!

Isaiah 26.19

O Death, where are your plagues? O Sheol, where is your destruction?

Hosea 13.14

For as in Adam all die, so also in Christ shall all be made alive... As it is written, "Death is swallowed up in victory. O death, where is thy victory? O death, where is thy sting?"

1 Corinthians 15.22 & 54-55

And I heard a loud voice from the throne saying, "Behold, the dwelling of God is with men... and they shall be his people; and God himself will be with them; he will wipe away every tear from their eyes, and death shall be no more, neither shall there be mourning nor crying nor pain anymore, for the former things have passed away."

Revelation 21.3-4

MESSIANIC KING

I saw in the night visions, and behold, with the clouds of heaven there came on like a Son of Man, and he came to the Ancient of Days and was presented before him. And to him was given dominion and glory and kingdom, that all peoples, nations and languages should serve him; his dominion is an everlasting dominion, which shall not pass away, and his kingdom is one that shall not be destroyed.

Daniel 7.13-14

The Lord is king, he is robed in majesty; the Lord is robed, he is girded with strength.

Psalm 93.1

And the angel said... "He will be great, and will be called the Son of the Most High; and the Lord God will give to him the throne of his father David, and he will reign over the house of Jacob forever; and of his kingdom there will be no end."

Luke 1.30 & 32-33

"My kingdom is not of this world."

John 18.36

ANCIENT OF DAYS

As I looked, thrones were placed and one that was Ancient of Days took his seat; his raiment was white as snow, and the hair of his head like pure wool; his throne was fiery flames, its wheels were burning fire.

Daniel 7.9

In the year that King Uzziah died I saw the Lord sitting upon a throne, high and lifted up; and his tram filled the temple, Above him stood the seraphim; each had six wings: with two he covered his face and with two he covered his feet, and with two he flew. and one called to another and said: "Holy, holy, holy is hte Lord of hosts; the whole earth is full of his glory."

Isaiah 6.1-3

A throne stood in heaven, with one seated on the throne... and round the throne, on each side of the throne, are four living creatures... each of them with six wings, full of eyes all around and within, and day and night they never cease to sing, "Holy, holy, holy is the Lord God Almighty, who was, who is and who is to come!"

Revelation 4.2, 6 & 8

And
he said to me,
"It is done! I am
the Alpha and the
Omega, the Beginning
and the End."

Revelation
21.6